It was Dad's turn to do the washing.

1

He put the sheets in the
washing machine.

"I need *all* the washing *now*!"
he shouted.

Kipper got his washing and
so did Chip.

"Put it down there," said Dad.

"I will do it in a bit," said Biff.

Biff had a look at her PE kit.
It had mud on it.

"This needs washing," she said.

"Well, put it in the washing machine," said Mum.

Biff put the PE kit in and Mum
went to turn it on.

All the green ran out of Biff's shorts.

Oh no! All the washing was green.

"Oh dear!" said Mum. "I did
not mean this to happen."

"Well, I think green sheets look good," said Mum.

Biff took her PE kit to school.

"Well, I think my green kit looks good," said Biff.